David and the Giant

Fiona Veitch Smith

Illustrations by Amy Warmington

SPCK

First published in Great Britain in 2012 by Crafty Publishing
Newcastle-upon-Tyne

This edition published in Great Britain in 2015

Society for Promoting Christian Knowledge
36 Causton Street
London SW1P 4ST
www.spck.org.uk

British Library Cataloguing-in-Publication Data
A catalogue record for this book is available from the British Library

ISBN 978–0–281–07457–0

10 9 8 7 6 5 4 3 2 1

Printed in Great Britain by Micropress

Produced on paper from sustainable forests

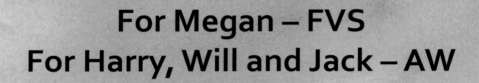

For Megan – FVS
For Harry, Will and Jack – AW

David was the **youngest** of **seven brothers** and **two sisters,**

who lived with their **mum and dad**

on a **very busy farm** near Bethlehem.

David was in charge of
looking after sheep,

and although it was an
important job,

he **had only** been given it

because **his brothers** had **better things** to do.

David's **brothers** were all **big** and **strong**

and, in their **spare time**, they practised fighting **with swords . . .**

throwing their spears . . .

and **shooting** their **bows and arrows.**

David's brothers

all wanted to fight in

the army,

so when a war broke out between

the **Israelites** and the **Philistines**

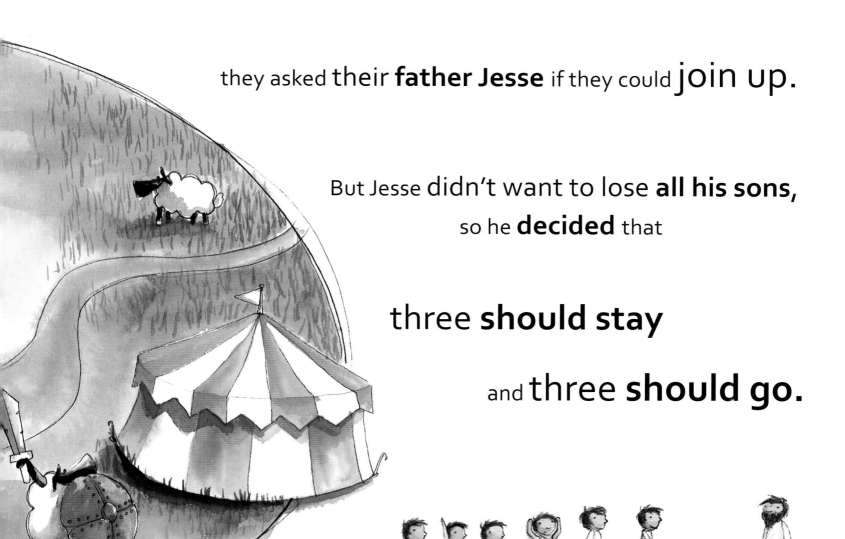

they asked their **father Jesse** if they could join up.

But Jesse didn't want to lose **all his sons**,
so he **decided** that

three **should stay**

and three **should go.**

"Eliab, Abinadab and Shammah –

you **three** are the **eldest**. Go and join **King Saul**
on the **battlefield** against the Philistines."

"**Yaaay**," said the three **eldest brothers**;

"**Naaay**,"  said the three youngest;

and **poor David,**

who hadn't even been counted,
said nothing.

A few days later, David's mum and **sisters,** Zeruaiah and Abigail,

gave him a huge basket of **food** to take to his brothers on the battlefield.

There were **sausages** and dried meat and loaves of bread and fruit and vegetables, and all sorts of yummy cakes and sweets.

David was very tempted to **try** some of it, **but he knew** if he did, his mum would **make him wash the dishes** for a month.

So David **climbed on a donkey**

and **rode to where** the Israelites were **fighting** the Philistines.

But the **donkey was**

soooooooooo slow.

"Hurry up", said **David,** "or we'll miss the action".

David was convinced that the **Israelites** would beat the **Philistines** in no time.

After all, they had **God** on their side.

David knew God **very well.**

He **talked** to Him
when he was **sitting alone**
watching the sheep,

singing them

songs

he had **made up**
on the harp.

David **remembered** the night **God had filled** him up with **courage,** when he had been **too scared** to face the **Hairy Beast.**

He knew that if Israel's army had **only half** of what **God had given him,** they would **send the Philistines home crying to their mummies.**

But, when David got to the battlefield, it was nothing like he imagined.

On one side of the valley were the Philistines, laughing and joking and having a great time;

on the **other side** were
the Israelites,

moping and moaning

and having a **miserable time.**

Every so often, a **giant man** would **walk out** of the **Philistine camp** and **stand in front** of the Israelites and **laugh.**

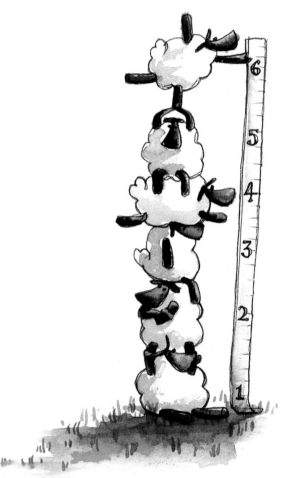

His name was **Goliath,**
and he was as tall as **6 fat sheep standing** on top of one another.

And when **Goliath walked**, the **whole earth** shook; and when **Goliath spoke**, the **whole world covered its ears**.

(not to scale)

"Who will fight me?" boomed **Goliath**.

"Is your God not strong enough to help you?"

But **not a single** Israelite stood up and said,

By this time **David** had found his brothers hiding **behind a rock.**

"Why won't anyone **fight him**?" asked David.

"How can you let him say **such terrible things** about **our God?"**

"Have you seen how **BIG** he is?" **asked Eliab.**

"There is **no one** in the Israelite camp **strong enough** to **fight him.**"

"Then I will **fight him,**" said David. But his brothers **just laughed.**

So **David** went to see King Saul who was **hiding** in a tent.

"But you are **just a boy,**" said the king.

"How **will you** fight this **giant?**"

"**God** will give me **strength,**"

said David and told the king about his **battle**

with the **Hairy Beast** that had tried to steal his father's sheep.

24

So the **king agreed** and made David put on some very **heavy** armour.
But the armour was **too heavy,** and poor David could hardly walk.

"Thanks but no thanks,"

said David.

"I'll just go as I am."

So **David went to fight** the giant in **nothing but** his everyday clothes.

He didn't have a **sword** and he **didn't have a shield,**

and the Philistines **just laughed** at him.

But David had some weapons that they couldn't see!

A **catapult,** a bag of stones and a great big powerful **God!**

"Come here and I will tear your arms and legs off!"

boomed Goliath.

But David wasn't scared.

He prayed a **prayer** . . .

put a **stone** in his **catapult** . . .

pulled it back and hurled it between the **giant's beady eyes.**

He **wibbled,** then he **wobbled,** then he **fell to the ground** with a bone shattering crash.

Goliath, the giant of the Philistines, **was dead.**

The Israelites **cheered** and
called David **their hero,**

then **picked up their swords**
and **chased** the rest of
the Philistines away.

David and the Giant is the third in the
Young David series.

Other books in the series:

David and the Hairy Beast
ISBN 978 0 281 07455 6

David and the Kingmaker
ISBN 978 0 281 07456 3

David and the Lonely Prince
ISBN 978 0 281 07458 7

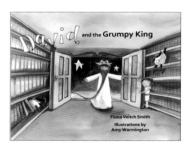

David and the Grumpy King
ISBN 978 0 281 07459 4

**David and the
Never-ending Kingdom**
ISBN 978 0 281 07460 0

www.spck.org.uk
http://fiona.veitchsmith.com